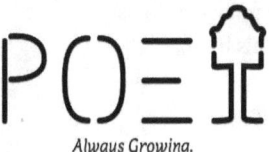

Always Growing.

Engineered by Poetree Brand
Creative Agency.
4125 South Figueroa Street
Los Angeles, CA, 90037
Email: Poetreebrand@gmail.com

Poetree Brand Creative Agency
Copyright 2017
Creative Direction: Poetree Brand
Book Design Layout by: Sean Slaughter
Cover Design: Sean Slaughter

published 2017.

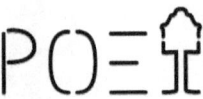

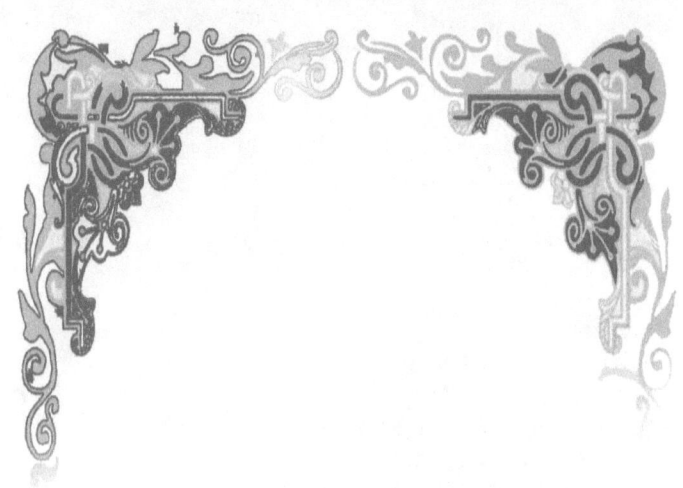

FOR MAYA,

AND THE DUST
ON THE PEOPLE'S
BOOKSHELVES

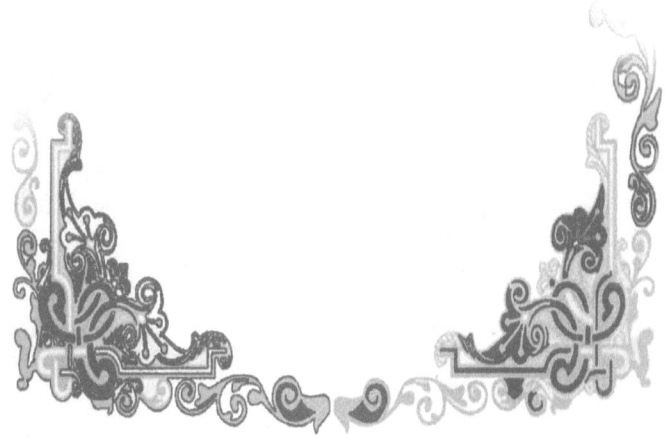

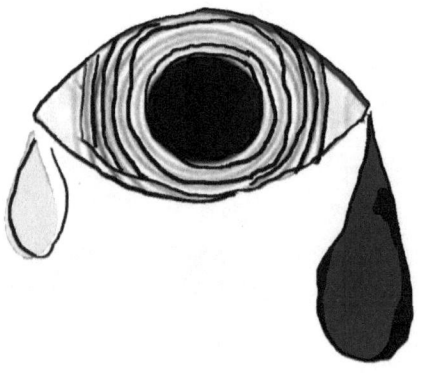

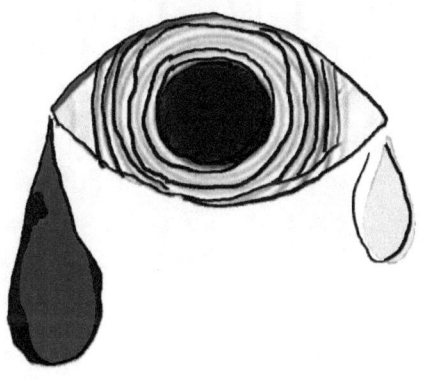

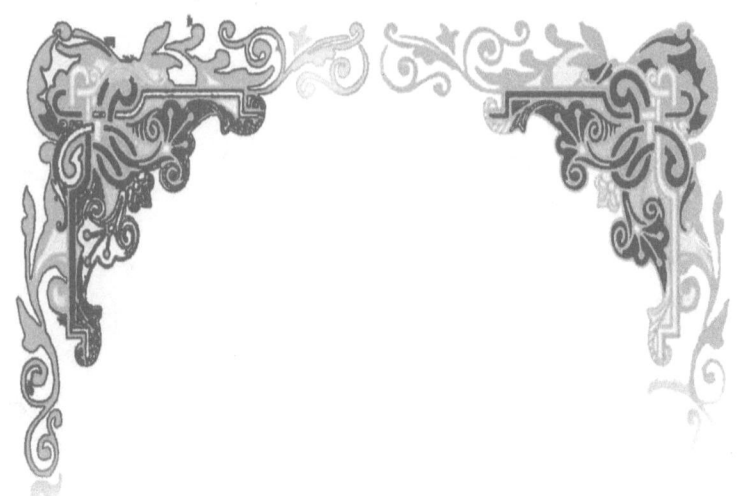

THAT WE MIGHT CRY SOUL TOGETHER

An Epic POEM
By: Kyle Sutherland

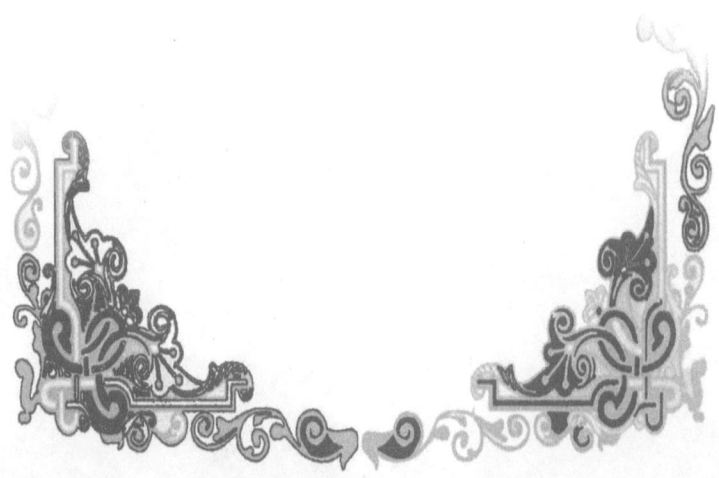

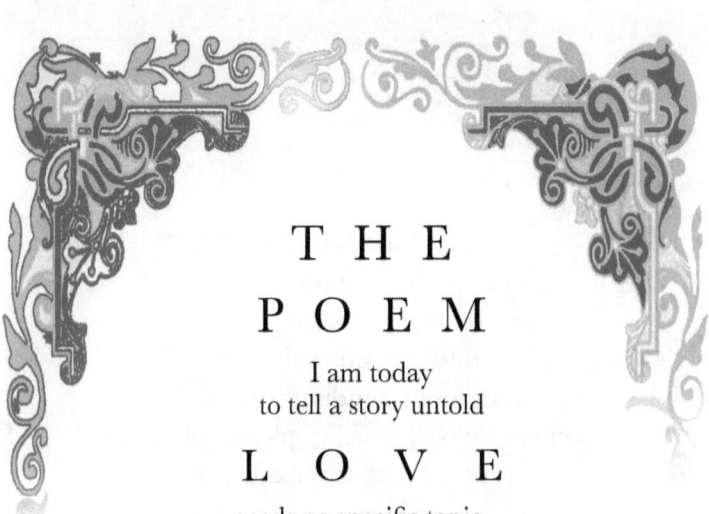

THE
POEM

I am today
to tell a story untold

L O V E

needs no specific topic,
only the written, living face of
reflection herself.
There is an inward rabbit
hole in every turn of events,
the most peculiar
reality is,

W h a t   W e   F e e l .

Part love story.
Part revolution song.
Part moonlight dream ramble.
Parts and pieces.
...the story,

The Dream.

Brush stroke & sleep on
riverbeds flow.

We are huddled,
humbled the poor living
dying life dancing soul
into city sidewalk rain
puddles pretending we are air
somebody well worthy, please join us &
report on all this exuberant
pain

can you hear our music?
do you feel
the bass in the heartbeat hit you?
where are all the lovers?
Our Love is closer,
the moon is following me.
I keep hearing her

whispering music,
leading me down the high grass
fox trails, I follow
on graveyards forgotten.

there is a winding staircase,
in your heart,
leading to a room of moonlight
an old ancestral box
you inherited

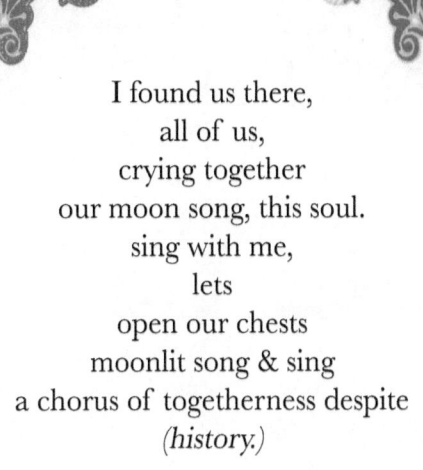

I found us there,
all of us,
crying together
our moon song, this soul.
sing with me,
lets
open our chests
moonlit song & sing
a chorus of togetherness despite
(history.)

despite the blood,
prisons like bombs,
like slaves like empire malicious and rabid
likes on facebook unlike
or follow to unfollow

much too much
like how our earth cries
this pain is stored as deep caverns
gems, our souls to live light the
(grit) (our)
story we *(die)*
to live.

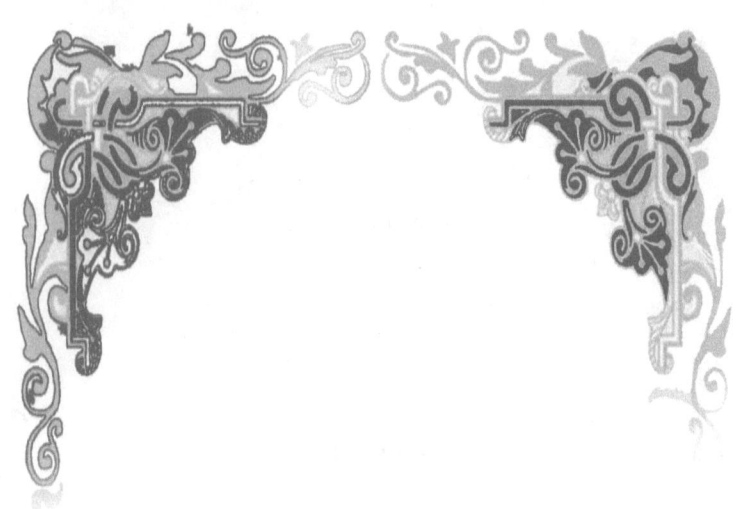

TO
LIGHT UP
FROM
WITHIN

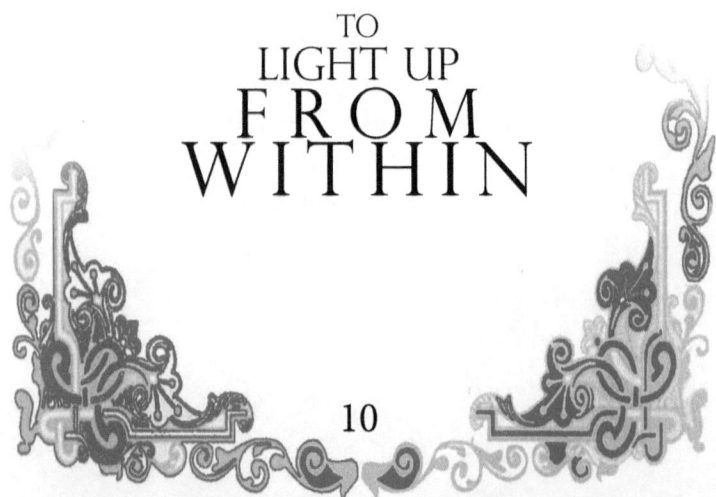

Look!

another human metropolis
all full throttle blur of opinions
and text messages, walls of solid masonry,
complicated wiring
Majesty...Love...Parks...Shootings...Dreams
netflix glow from windows
in modern highrises

morning feet stomp unison anthill
and fingers phone endless scroll down
like when the traffic jams
the city into a boombox -
and elsewhere
all here bombs drop

the pain tells
stories like text messages
of the ancient texts unfold

..break down your
barriers, O Dying Life
feel one another more deeply,

L O V E

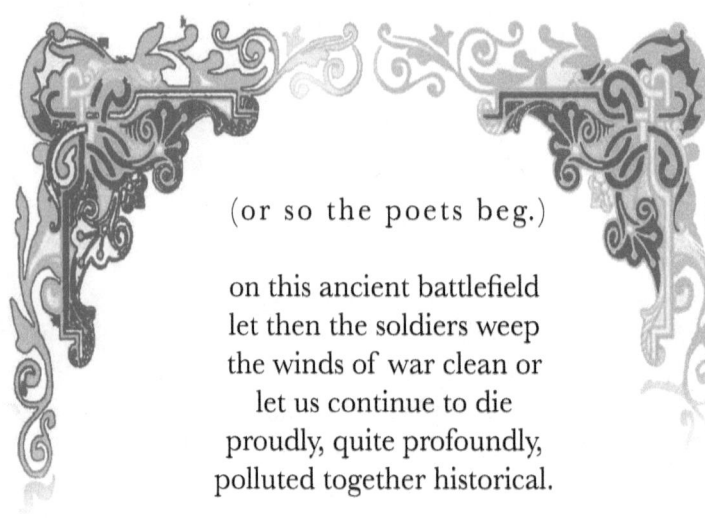

(or so the poets beg.)

on this ancient battlefield
let then the soldiers weep
the winds of war clean or
let us continue to die
proudly, quite profoundly,
polluted together historical.

& but
H e r - S t o r y
is.
M u s t   n e e d s   b e   t o l d.
...
that we might
c r y   s o u l   t o g e t h e r
...my heart is full
of womens stories
birthing all memory
of thought, my wife
is a distance I cannot reach
but our pinkies ring forever
in our hearts,

a   v o w   o f   h a n d s

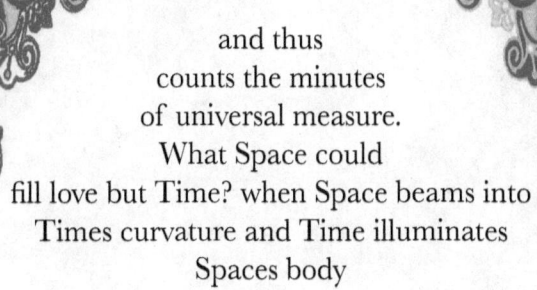

and thus
counts the minutes
of universal measure.
What Space could
fill love but Time? when Space beams into
Times curvature and Time illuminates
Spaces body

T h e   W o r l d

is roses lavender silk
my love and I live thus,
Thus;
when the war drums
start pounding
the walls tremble and say,

*"f i n d   y o u r   L o v e
p r o t e c t   h e r   b r e a t h"*

there is no distance
you cannot cross.

I am running home,

h e r   h a n d s,

through the meadows,
through the fog.

13

.chest.
.burning.

the city is lit. a heartbeat.
an electrical board.
little lantern palaces,
as headlights flicker.
mountain shadows,
when the cosmos blends.
& somewhere in the flux
I am running,
thinking this,

s u f f e r i n g
eating lifes sweet honey

dying shiny
waving at you
smiling at dead

s t a r s
s t i l l
s h i n i n g

The worlds overflowing glow.
I am writing this,

is written
that you may read it into Being read
step out of the shadows,
O
you who
will
never
read
this.

I am in the shadows,
with all the poetry
I will never read

what will you fill your souls cup with ?
my heart is a golden lamp
of purple mixed love
with blue light green
& red shadows cast
of actors dancing
songstresses emcees
hippies punks
full of coal mines labor
and collective tears
I've collected for this occasion.
for us to cry soul.

have you ever listened
to the Way of
Heart is color?
every stories shade...
living miracle of...

can the language serve as a ladder to a
moonlight within?
when you hear it
the high notes
can you see it moving light
to echo forever?

...pain...
...love...

if then language the ladder
let then it also be
the hammer the wing tip
the graveyard, the future
if then it be those things
how best to express...
how should it go?
...it should go
without saying
and so, be.
Here, hear this,

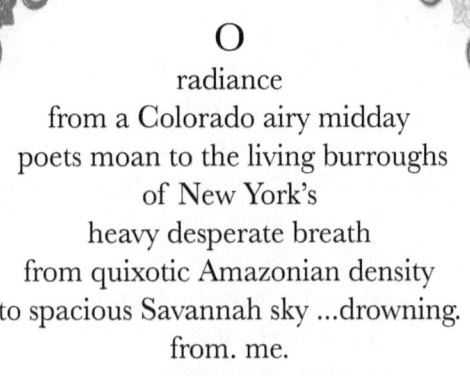

O
radiance
from a Colorado airy midday
poets moan to the living burroughs
of New York's
heavy desperate breath
from quixotic Amazonian density
to spacious Savannah sky ...drowning.
from. me.
to. you.

d r o w n i n g .

souls mountains as close as voice
poems & letters. future memories.
chapbooks n' scrapbooks.
Pictures of us kissing my Love,
written future present now.
The Love
worldwide under siege. Forever. Strong.
... find your souls mountains,
climb meet me there
with your ancestral box of moonlight
with blueprints of new worlds
and heavens.
& havens.
& songs.

Today is the birthday
of everywhere. We sing a
blessing. We tell our
grandmothers & grandfathers
we love them. Today we forget ourselves.
And kingdom come

Today come tomorrow and dance
today a revolution brews
ugly fermented dreams
entire cities, fall.
Winter of our hearts.
forests.

The wolves are howling here
we are spring leaf,
is new life moon spun

(as every mother is every
mother is you being born)

summer circles a holy cycle.
Genderless light is shining
on today, today
the black boy died again.
The cop cruiser drove off,
written - unsentenced.

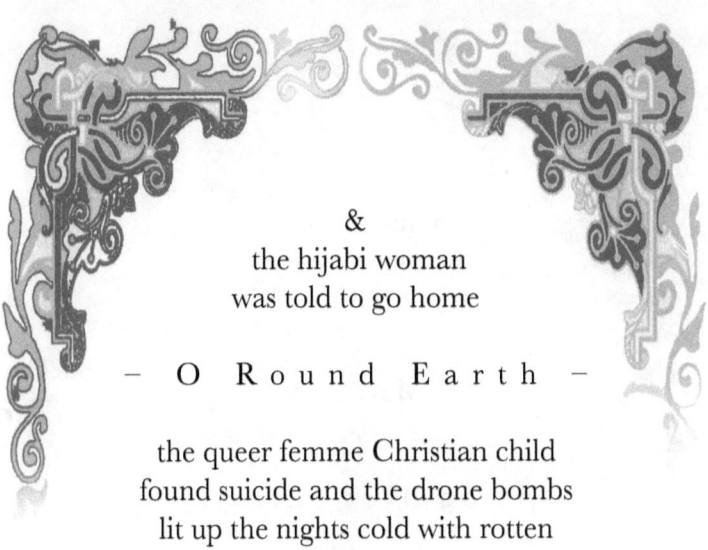

&
the hijabi woman
was told to go home

– O R o u n d E a r t h –

the queer femme Christian child
found suicide and the drone bombs
lit up the nights cold with rotten
Devil breath,

L a u g h i n g .

the empires fell into our faces.

L a u g h i n g .

pointing in circles.

if that you could Remember
what matters is Love

-

virtues triumph beauty in the soul
mixes personality to snowflake imprints

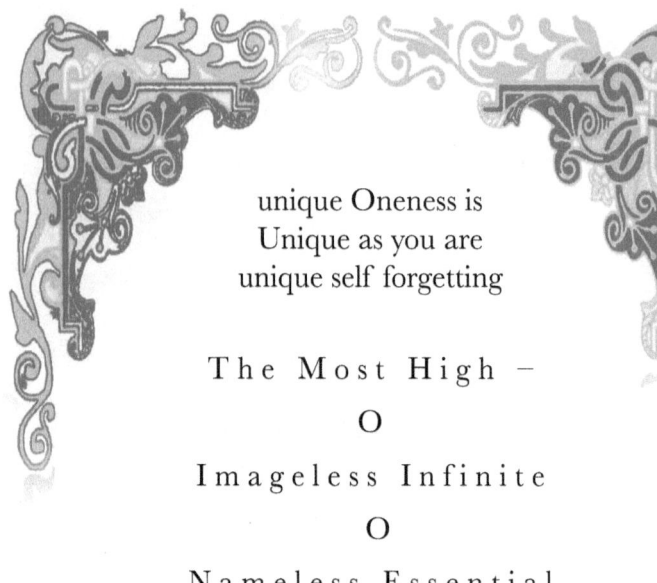

unique Oneness is
Unique as you are
unique self forgetting

The Most High –

O

Imageless Infinite

O

Nameless Essential

what does it mean to
forget life self
is sacred?
I am at your doorstep
with flowers

O

Round Earth

with the density of words,
all hiding without boundaries
running laps, circular
life circles itself
holy sacred these
flowers whither

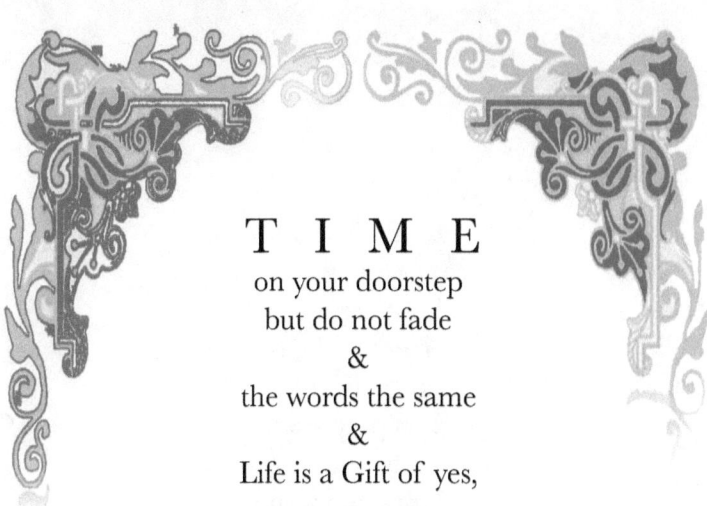

T I M E

on your doorstep
but do not fade
&
the words the same
&
Life is a Gift of yes,

Y E S .

death is an angel.
appointment, imminent.
& so,
while living the human gift of

y e s

look me in your eyes,
gifted stars we share
see you in my vision
I see me in your eyes
any time I look
&

We are here.

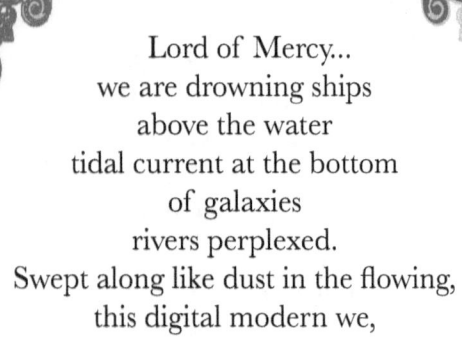

Lord of Mercy...
we are drowning ships
above the water
tidal current at the bottom
of galaxies
rivers perplexed.
Swept along like dust in the flowing,
this digital modern we,

my analogue
ancient love, our land at sea.
A forest folded into
this living poems heart

O

today the trees
declare themselves once again
steadfast
will you stand alongside
your breath tree bound
roots declarative & steadfast ?

Solidarity is breathing with.
So please,
indulge.

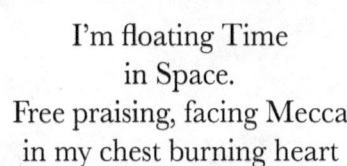

I'm floating Time
in Space.
Free praising, facing Mecca
in my chest burning heart

Beloved
crossing the aegis of rusty minds
canoeing with elders
in a dream-web of stories
untold
sailing wayward into wisdoms
center

last night of the world
a generation burned up,
burned out
we took lysergic acid,
smiled ancient memories,
sat by subwoofers
smoked ourselves dizzy
imaginings
and
here we are
.ghosts.

.living. .symbols.
we know what we know.
have known. soul.
We trip out on futures Afro and Dreams
of that vision is
Hashtag; stay woke & sleep city dreams
visions awake,
nights days times suns moons rays
reflected here

Here

is our anniversary, of going so
wonderfully mad begging for people
to feel. Soul.
To Weep. Feeling. Soul. Reep. Sowed. Love.
Garden. Gravity. Of. Heart.

Living

the city dreams
of first days of
lush forests but
then forests remember & lament
the cities toxic (masculine) touch
but...you knew that...

(and you left your beer can
in the forest anyway)

Toxic Men
in an ocean of

SHE is Divine

young girls in Palestine
dream of Eternal Love
&
scud missiles dream differently
...echoes in Syria...
&
somewhere someone folds their arms
shakes their head at the mention of
Palestine or Syria

O

but have you cried
for the dead of Iraq or Afghanistan,
point out which dead civilian was your
enemy

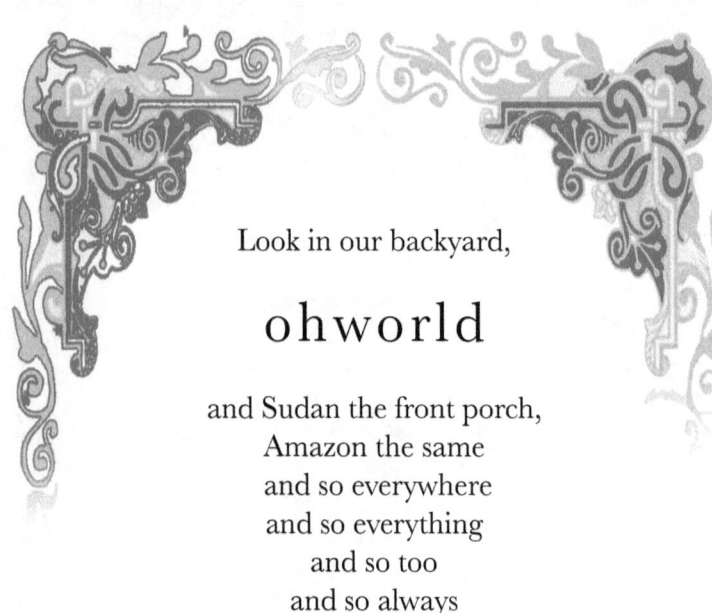

Look in our backyard,

ohworld

and Sudan the front porch,
Amazon the same
and so everywhere
and so everything
and so too
and so always
.and so.

. C r y .
. S o u l .

If you fight
for freedom
then every fight
for freedom
is your fight.
Live up,
feel more

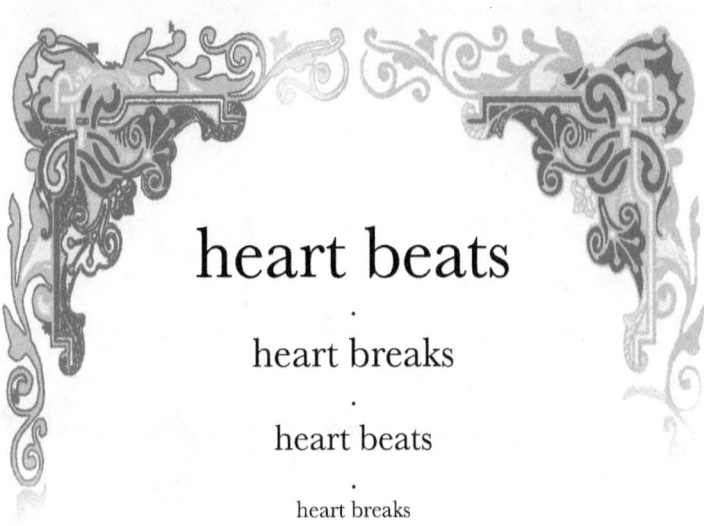

heart beats

.

heart breaks

.

heart beats

.

heart breaks

.

b r e a k b e a t   m y   h e a r t

My Love, My Love!
The tears have fallen oceans
around my fire
Let's run
Space....
….......is
running......
out......
…......here
is.....
Time....
….left
….......for
few...
dreams..........

27

Get on the Train with me,
M y   L o v e ,
M y   L o v e !

after the engines halt,
the workers step like clockwork
onto the platform
simultaneous to us –
this living story,
my love
dip your holy-have-traveled-feet
into the blue pool
of
M y   L o v e ,   M y   L o v e !

Clockwork
Time.
Platform
Space.
Herstory and History
Space blends Time watercolor
...blood red
read the blues
we put our fists up.
the tanks smashed against
our bodies but
fists up

28

Revolution
Everlasts

is really just us saying peace now & always
let cultures thrive living to share human
the breathing chant testimony of please let
Earth be the living Being She is YES!
let the Muslim pray covered to Most High,
O dream to let the Black Girl be Beautiful
Natural and let Lakota and Arapaho live
land of ancestry let the Dalai Lama die in
Tibet and let the tyrants fall cities with our
winter and stop plastic earth and advertise
our death misery we see right through it,
we've seen through it the whole time,
propaganda machine war drum eclipse the
sun bleeds our little hearts beat off tune
micro-nationalism and macro-economic
false messiah prevails the day is donzo and
so please read too deeply into this or not
enough so that this abstract perfection of
our recflected madness is just enough to
MADE IN CHINA denim pants our out of
shape Trumped American legs when
the bombs really hit, and the
war song becomes

Truly
Desperate

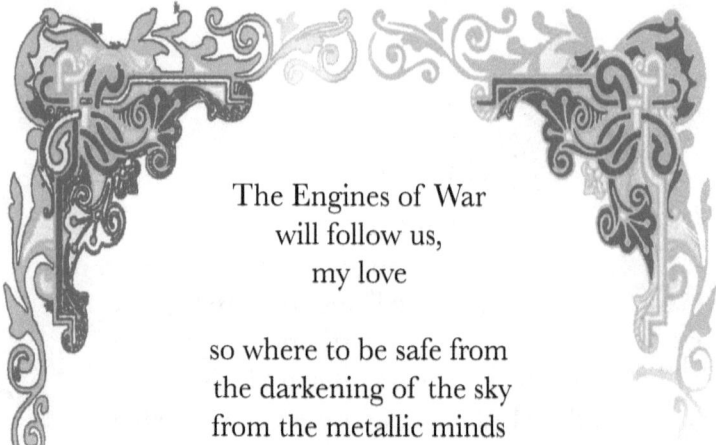

The Engines of War
will follow us,
my love

so where to be safe from
the darkening of the sky
from the metallic minds
iron frenzy from the climate

Herself,
mistreated,
woman – weeping
in love?

Where will we run, my love
when the city stops her hum
in favor of something
more simple? Love...
I ran into heaven,
on the street , her fist raised,
she said

"The Love you Found
lives lightbulbs within me,
you need no currency,
save for love,

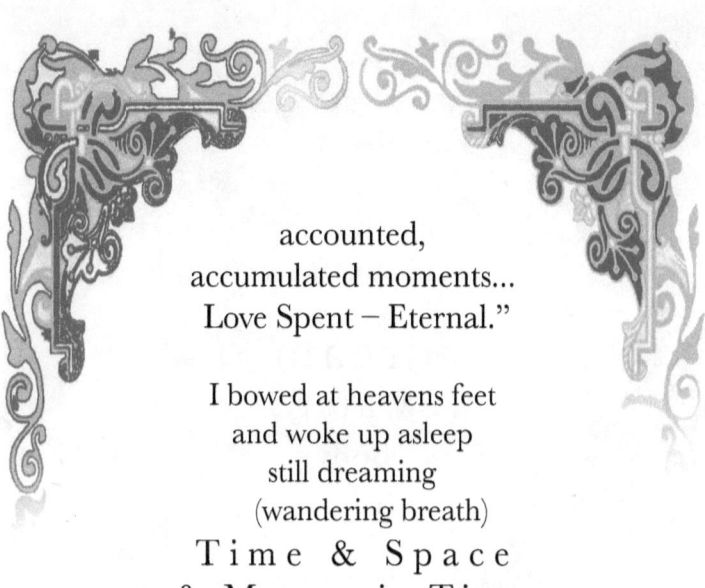

accounted,
accumulated moments...
Love Spent – Eternal."

I bowed at heavens feet
and woke up asleep
still dreaming
(wandering breath)
T i m e   &   S p a c e
&   M o n e y   i s   T i m e
currently not having any money
is destroying my life
...
all the money having
destroying the worlds life
so take this labor
callous these hands
humble work for
tablescraps
and empty pocket
dance in rain puddles

All Soul, So Here Now
As the Rain is as Pour/Poor
Down as we are

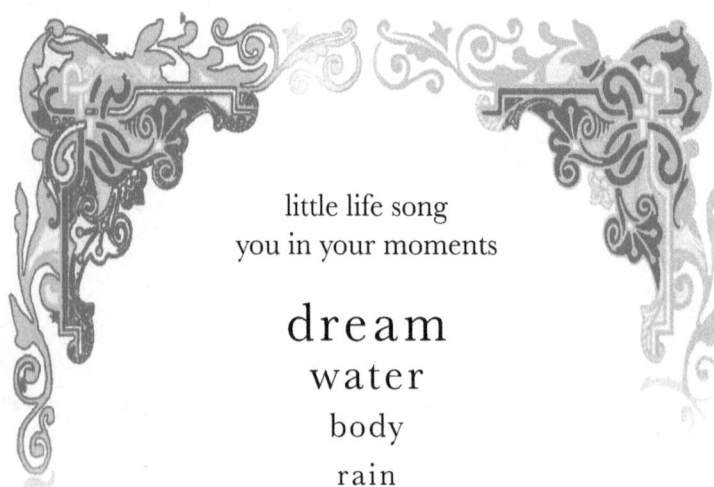

little life song
you in your moments

dream
water
body

rain

puddles, I am & only want to be out
standing, asleep across the world,
looking up at rain, puddles rain fall
while my love bathes in water falls
while the war rages fire fights
her oceans calm within;
outstanding.

Give us

New scenes

in this Production
Love stands out theatrical

I found my love.
teaching patience to the child of my heart
she smiled entire rivers of medicine
healing she stands in
this heart where

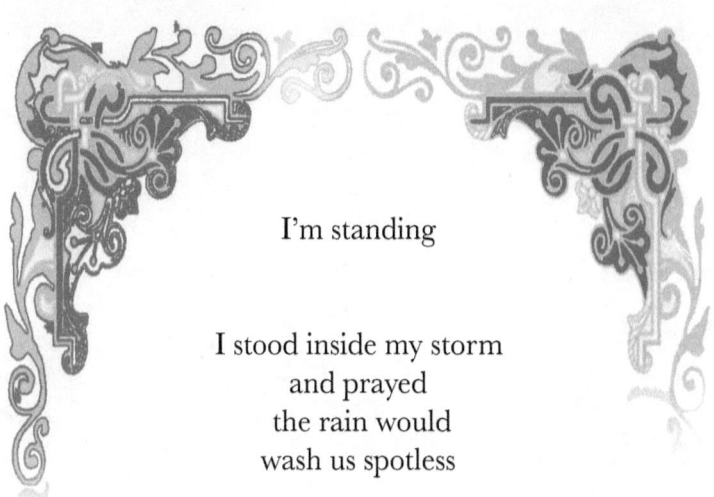

I'm standing

I stood inside my storm
and prayed
the rain would
wash us spotless

o u t s t a n d i n g.

outside,
I'm standing in your dream,
lightning...the forest burns
the weather treacherous,
sub Saharan African climate war heat,

O
L o v e

(have you listened to your carbon
footprintboot stomp on
soveriegn life elsewhere?)

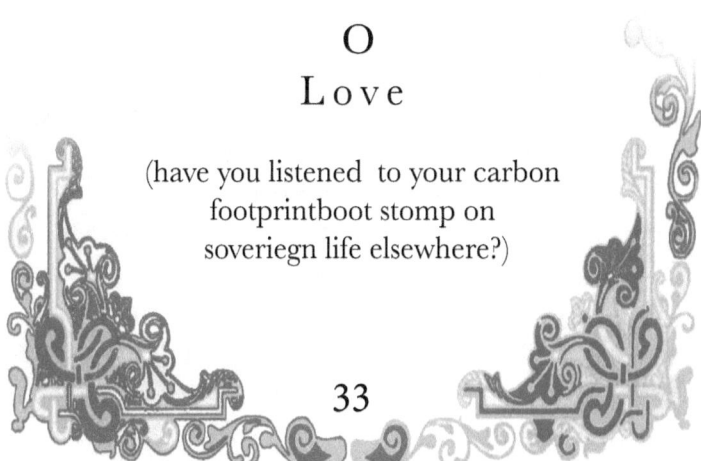

the smoke stacks
like pallets

we drink from plastic bottles
that kill seagulls at sea,
bodies washed, *ashore*
as patriots smash beer cans on their heads
and the bones of Buffalo
and Natives buried in soul

soil under our feet
turn into petrified wood
sold at high prices
rare relics,
fashionable
death.

O
L i f e
you thing...
Our Feeling.
our egos hard - rock a steady front
no one has our back.
smoke, crack the sky open
arms flailing
and bellies hungry

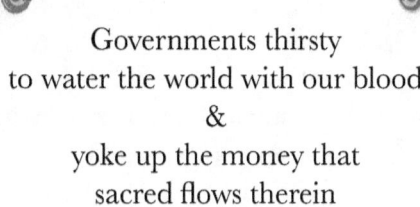

Governments thirsty
to water the world with our blood
&
yoke up the money that
sacred flows therein

&
whom then to work the soil?
Will you garden the gravity of air
by planting trees to breathe
the depth of breath?

...this
book of trees

T h i s
L i v i n g
B r e a t h
my poems are fallen trees
breathing my soul

crying
with us

a g a i n .

35

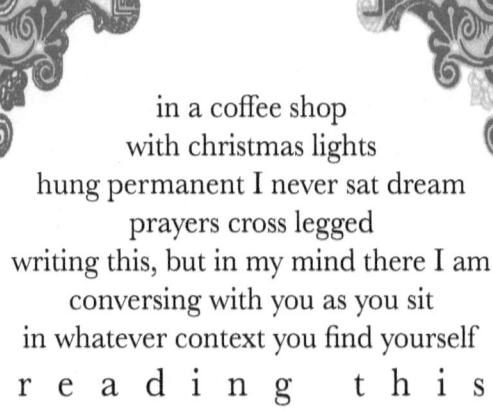

in a coffee shop
with christmas lights
hung permanent I never sat dream
prayers cross legged
writing this, but in my mind there I am
conversing with you as you sit
in whatever context you find yourself
r e a d i n g   t h i s

here, take a sip of this quadruple shot
espresso and wake up a bit,

d r e a m e r
the coffee is hot.

Our conversation
stamina suddenly
Jasmine Tea
in my dream and then
eucalyptus and the smell
of her coconut oil or rasberries
on a warm day
like the feeling of your hands
– right now-
or your heart
most importantly

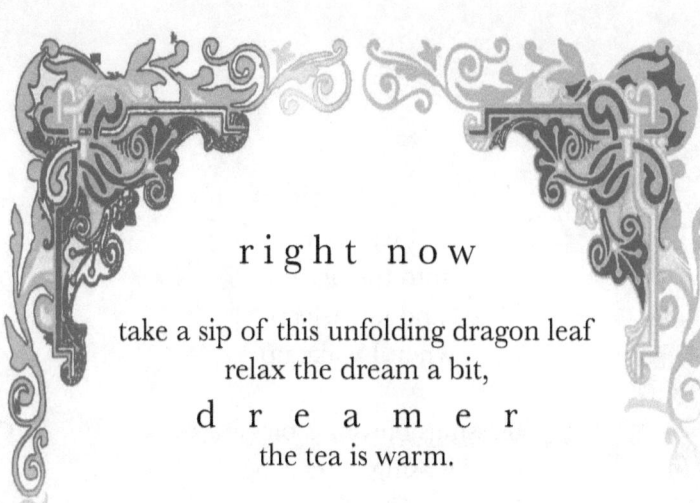

right now

take a sip of this unfolding dragon leaf
relax the dream a bit,
d r e a m e r
the tea is warm.

Our conversation
polite.

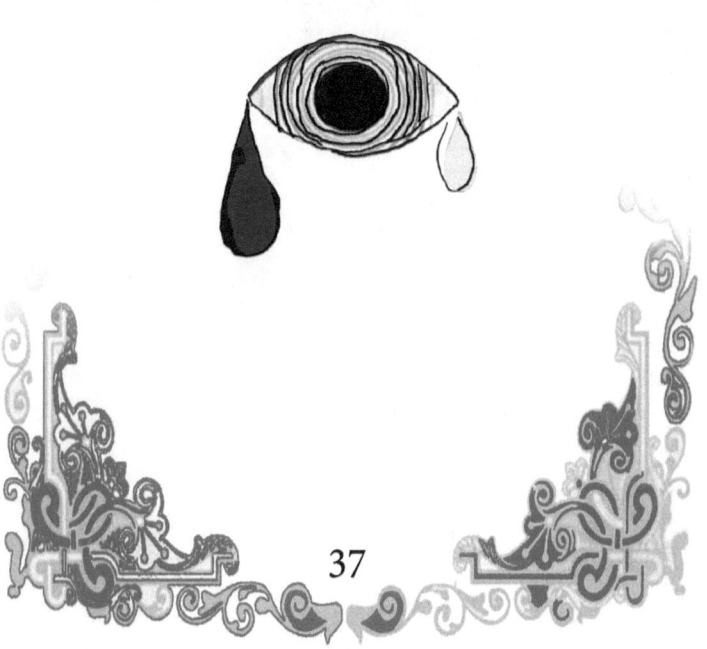

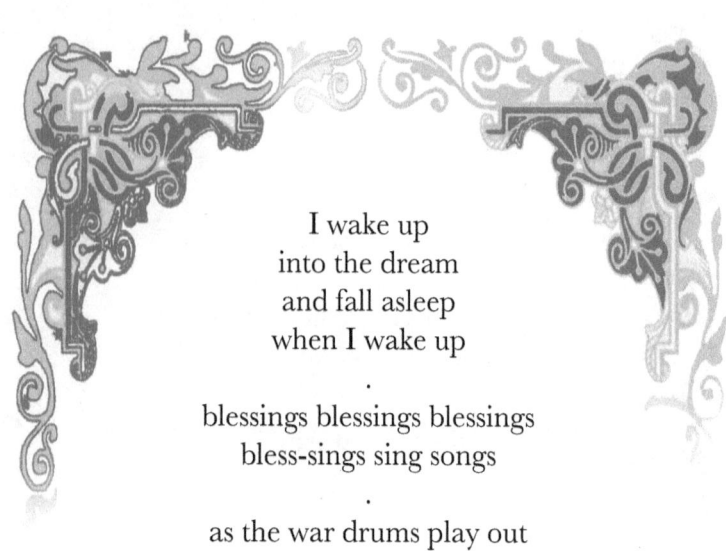

I wake up
into the dream
and fall asleep
when I wake up

.

blessings blessings blessings
bless-sings sing songs

.

as the war drums play out
the stage is all but still standing

.

whose bombs are these?
whose bullets, the one who loads them
or the one who recieves them like
plague?

whose dream
is this?

whose war
is this?

O
Round Earth

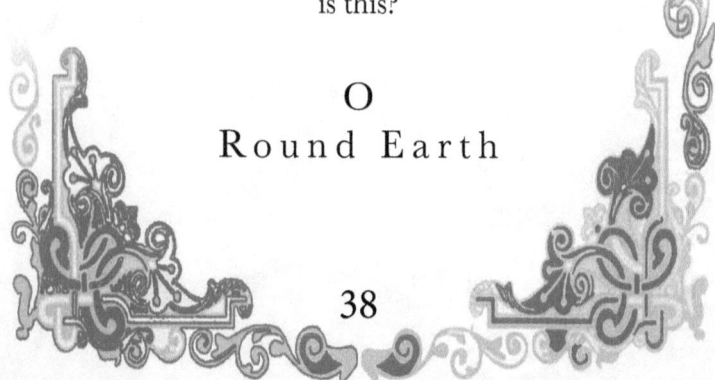

Will we wake up?
or sleep through
the storms claws?

children of the world,
this is your
dream life & death
vision

& I am only
a dream character
carrying you
to yourself
.Ageless.

we carry prisoners
home.

refugees in the mirror
of our market knotted souls

or

the sincere scarlet ever poetic thrust
of stories told,
hurts when untied like this

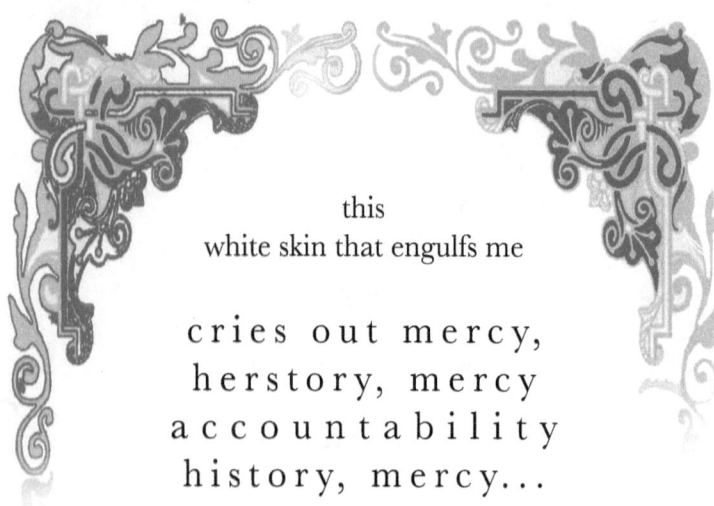

this
white skin that engulfs me

c r i e s   o u t   m e r c y ,
h e r s t o r y ,   m e r c y
a c c o u n t a b i l i t y
h i s t o r y ,   m e r c y . . .

this parade of empire
sick game on fast forward
souls
die
before
the body

Will you Not
Cry
Soul
with us?
O
Whiteness,
The Future is
Afro
A n c i e n t

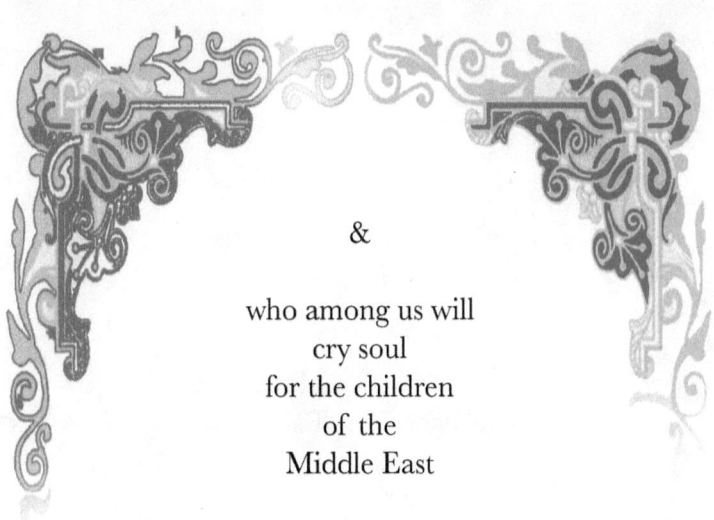

&

who among us will
cry soul
for the children
of the
Middle East

for
Africa's smile
for
Asia's song
for
here do you see
the homeless American child

O
Rich Man Walking
do you tread light
on this native land?

to cry for this
Self-Hood
…to hood

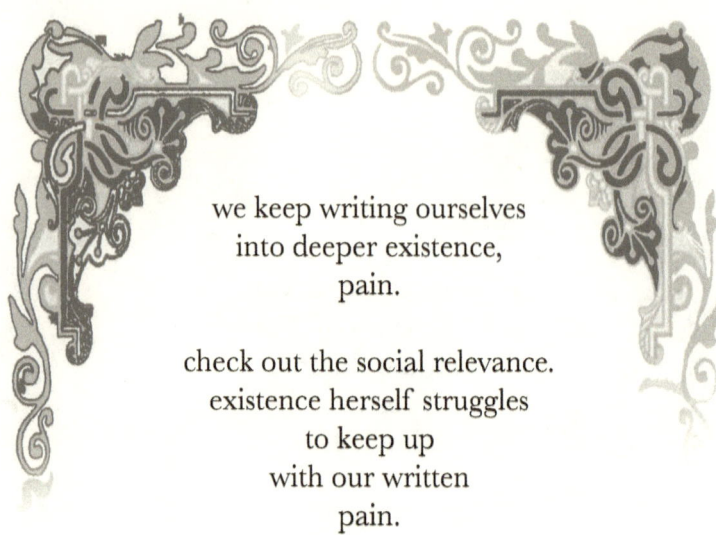

we keep writing ourselves
into deeper existence,
pain.

check out the social relevance.
existence herself struggles
to keep up
with our written
pain.

Check out the political relavance.
s o u l s   r e l e v a n t .

self checkout at the warehouse
we call a grocery store
check out this selfie,
I took it. My ego,
my generation our fire
the moment the actual moment,
money, trades barters whips chains
oceans polluted
we buy
more

keep
following...

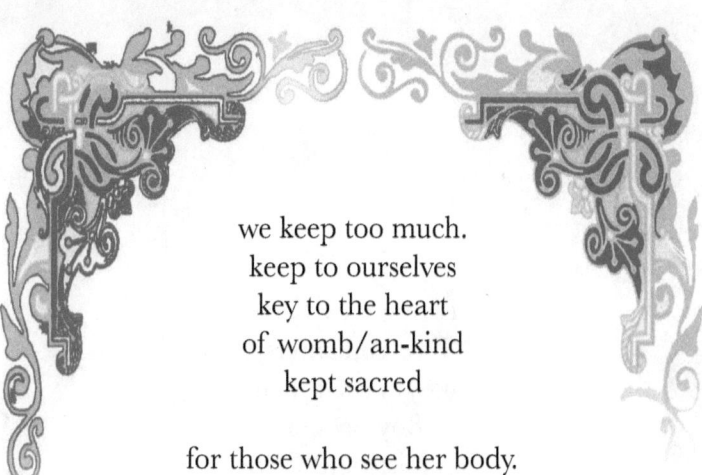

we keep too much.
keep to ourselves
key to the heart
of womb/an-kind
kept sacred

for those who see her body.
I keep waking up,
running chest burning
where is all the Time?
Gone?

My Love,
she is the whisp of
neon lights any every color all at once
or all eye caught
fascinated by her in this Life,
every any
Time

I caught her, facscinated, falling
− but I catch her
rising tide moonsong,
my war time
lullaby

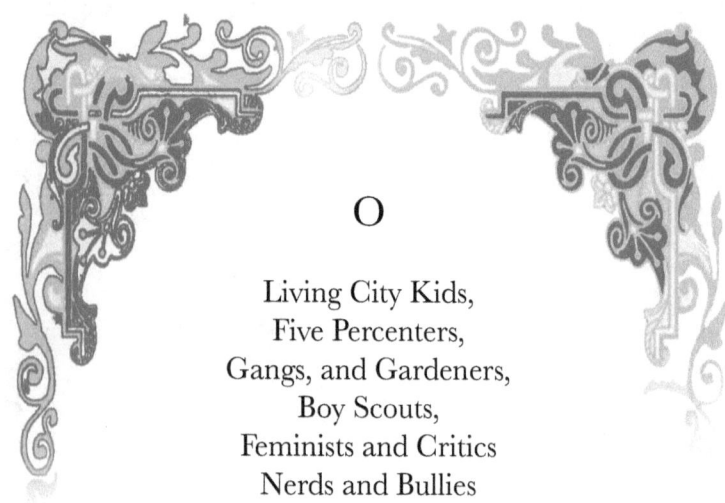

O

Living City Kids,
Five Percenters,
Gangs, and Gardeners,
Boy Scouts,
Feminists and Critics
Nerds and Bullies

Hear this, beat kick, ear drum,
boom bap, song sung,
slap you,

feel that
r e b e l   a n t h e m
(d y i n g)

hear this fist raised
royal purple rain down
cammo kick break down
(walls) living Raggae Music
Punk Music
Hip Hop

M u s i c

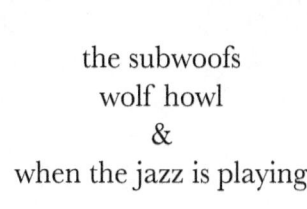

the subwoofs
wolf howl
&
when the jazz is playing

there's really
nothing to say
because

All We
Ever
Really Say

is just
all that

JAZZ

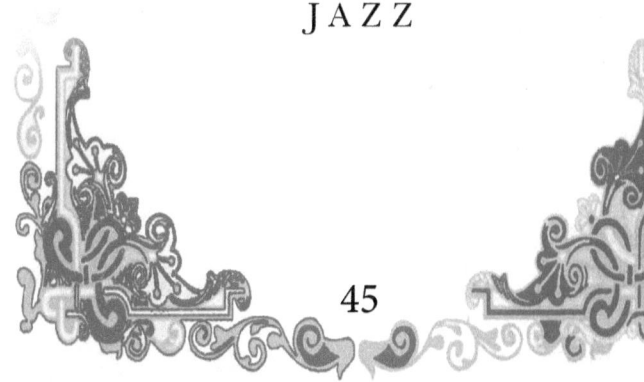

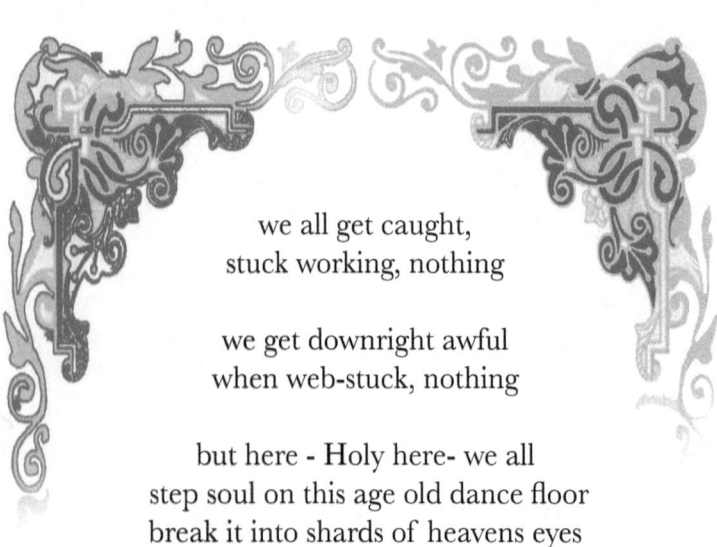

we all get caught,
stuck working, nothing

we get downright awful
when web-stuck, nothing

but here - Holy here- we all
step soul on this age old dance floor
break it into shards of heavens eyes

seeing in the rhythm
souls cry

seeing in the melody
spirits arise

seeing in the harmony
chakras firework

sight in the beat itself
hearts fire
works
over-time
over-times-turn-tables

Overturn the Tables,
Love

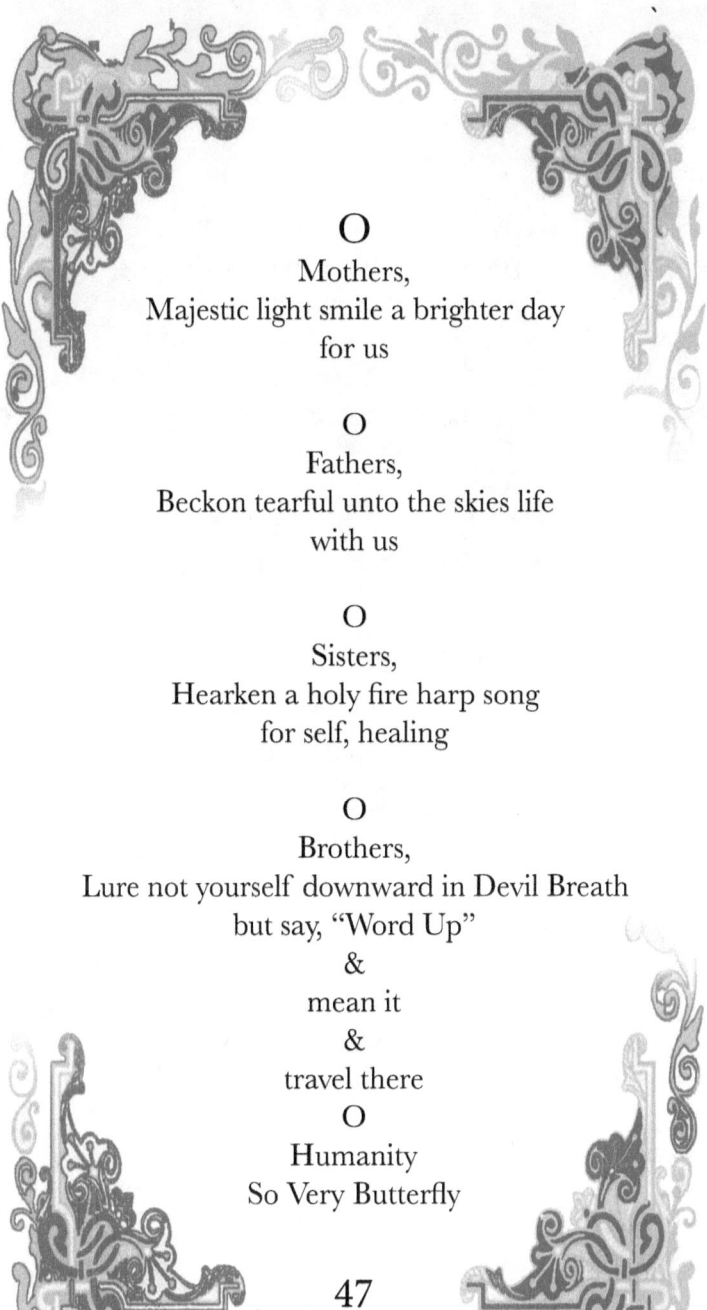

O

Mothers,

Majestic light smile a brighter day

for us

O

Fathers,

Beckon tearful unto the skies life

with us

O

Sisters,

Hearken a holy fire harp song

for self, healing

O

Brothers,

Lure not yourself downward in Devil Breath

but say, "Word Up"

&

mean it

&

travel there

O

Humanity

So Very Butterfly

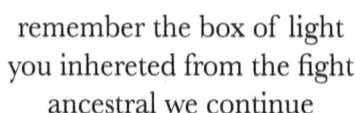

remember the box of light
you inhereted from the fight
ancestral we continue

use it against
the systems, crumble

after so much
death, we endure

how much light
can we share
to endure
our death
for life?

The Box is a circle of Moonlight,
is open to shine and light the way
The moon is following you
I keep hearing her music
telling you to follow the fox trails
you forgot in the cities
on graveyards

we forget

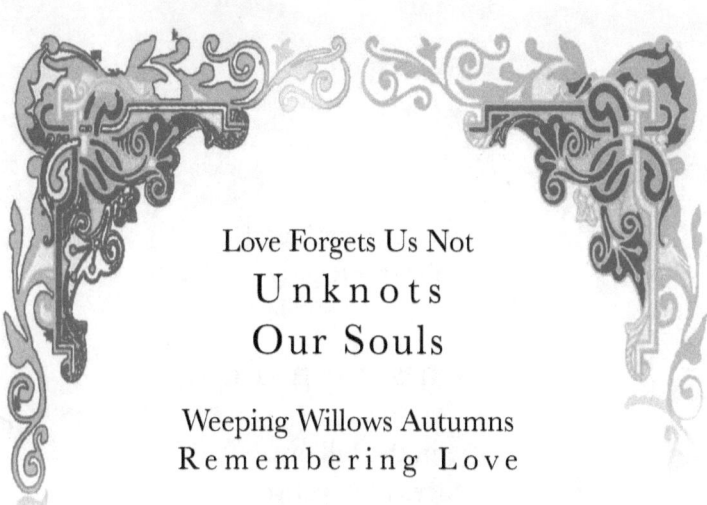

Love Forgets Us Not
Unknots
Our Souls

Weeping Willows Autumns
Remembering Love

Love Remembers
You Wept With Her

Genderless
Light

Shines

The Most High

Divine

Prayers and Offerings

Sacred
Life

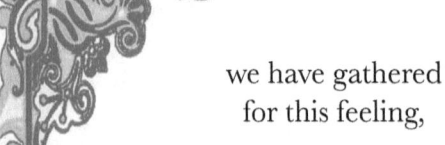

we have gathered
for this feeling,

T r a n s c e n d e n t

in the billions,
faces blur, yet you,
my love, are my love,
my love, take my hand

look down
at how short

.

T h e   F a l l

b u t   n o w

.

l o o k   u p

.

s e e ?

the villages seasons harvest is
the cities wayward movement,
is the inventor brilliant cooky,
is the readers here now heart,

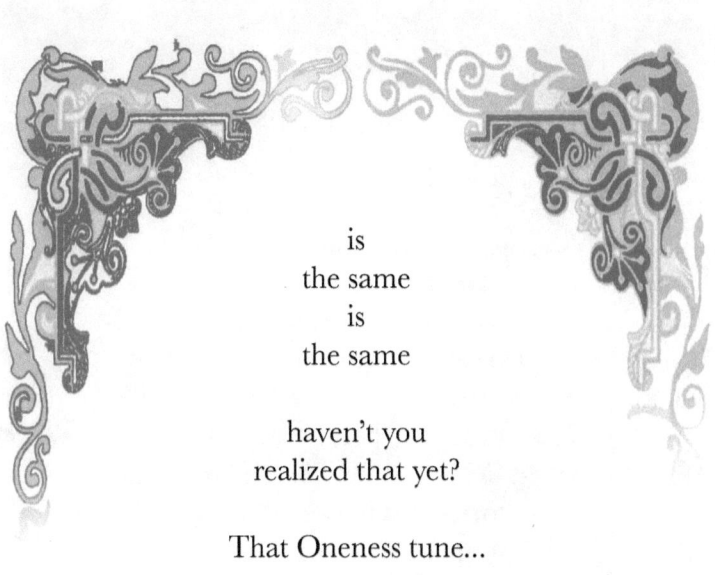

is
the same
is
the same

haven't you
realized that yet?

That Oneness tune...

...uniquely you...
...that you might
cry

.

in Awe

.

& delight tears, life

.

narrow passage

.

vast
horizon

.

living a
dying breath

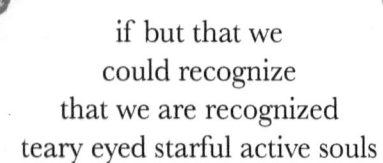

if but that we
could recognize
that we are recognized
teary eyed starful active souls

here
caught living this precipice of moment
stories told to each other...
some held untold graves.
the stories endless

the ones I could fiction
or non-fiction
or poem
the ones in you,
every word I cannot utter,
does not occur in me to say,
every story I will not live,
that place,
you,
the passing blur
the closest heart, this humanity
recognizes itself in the mirror
of a
Story,
living dreams

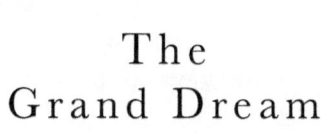

The Grand Dream

the one you live everyday
I am writing it alongside you

living it, living you,
this melodramatic ritual
life song and dance

the real fight against
the real fight for
trial and error backdrop

eternity
life and death
cycles breath
breathes sleep
dream awake vision.

w a k e u p.

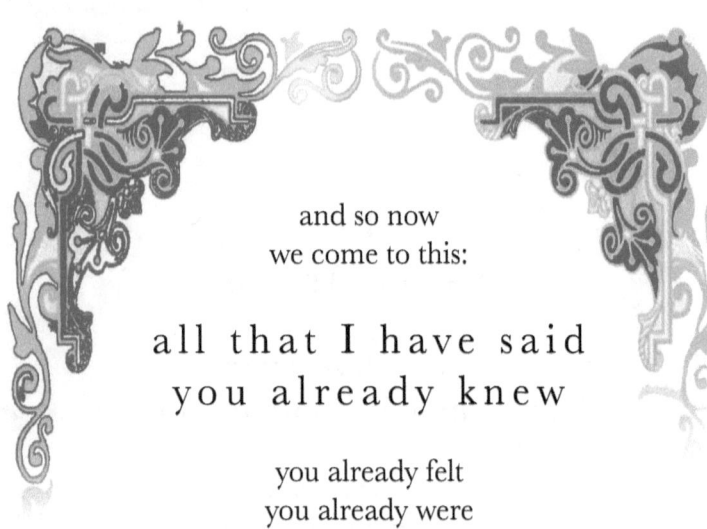

and so now
we come to this:

all that I have said
you already knew

you already felt
you already were

so what now?
Will you dream a grander dream,
dreamer?

To plant a garden...
to rally the people...
That box of light
is open
for you

the moon song

c r i e s   o u t
Answer the feeling,

is already
felt

the soul expession is
the soul rejoices when
the souls depth
cries out.

Remember the box the moonlight the
winter the hearts the circle the heavens the
fists up the rain the winding staircase the
dream the awake vision the feeling the
genderless light, The Time
she the Love of my Life, I Space
my life – your dream,

remember the the living dying moment the
war drums the dance floor the rain puddles
the city,the sky, the oceans, the lullaby,
the trees, the breath, the story untold,
the Afro future, the Ancient, the desperate
moment

c r y i n g
s o u l
t o g e t h e r

Here. Now.